£2.99

6A
/20

On the Seventh Wave

On the Seventh Wave

David Hodges

On the Seventh Wave

ISBN 9780956688439
Acknowledgements
Spirituality, Religious Life Review,
The Merton Journal and The Merton Seasonal
in which some of these poems first appeared

Published by The Abbey, Caldey Island,
Tenby, Pembs. SA70 7UH. Wales, G.B.

On the Seventh Wave

On the Seventh Wave

Cast off, let slip
into the grip of the unknown,
swift on the seventh wave
of the breaking tide,
into the sea's inviting arms.
Safe for now
in its gently rolling waves,
running free before the wind;
now free but subject
to the random wildness
of its many moods.

In the Flight of Birds

The breaking waves, the spray,
seabirds in the changing light;
over the passing years
I've learnt their music—

in the flight of birds
to the setting sun, begun
to learn what unseen beauty,
what secrets, lie beyond.

Starlings

Starlings exploding
from dry grass, regrouping,
diving, dipping, tumbling
over drystone walls,
spiralling in the sunlight,
eager to show off
their fancy moves
and disappearing tricks;
wheeling, swooping, turning
in a seeming orchestrated whole,
as I, transfixed, delight in heart and soul—
and all their fun and play today
more praise to God than my attempts to pray.
The earth has this and other wonders
that continuously unfold.

Gypsy Cobs in the Lighthouse Field

Ponies stood in profile, on the rise,
black silhouettes, majestic
against the darkening skies.
Clouds scudding, clashing,
riding the gusting squalls.

Trying to outrun the wind,
ponies racing, frisky, fighting,
manes flicking, swishing tails,
joyful in the blowing gales
and, now, a brightening sky.

Overhead cables wildly swaying,
then a zip, like a crack of a whip;
sparks fly, ponies circle and scatter,
as if half remembering a trick
or a scene from some old routine.

Welsh Gypsy Cobs

Sally, Beti, Mix Up,
Smokey, Pepper, Peanut.
Coats of dun and smoky black,
black and chestnut;
white blaze, white hooves,
one with plaited fringe,
one all black, one with hooves
all oddly different colours.

By the bothy, shy and hiding,
now moving gently closer;
friendly, trusting,
backs glistening, gleaming,
steaming in the sunlight;
alert, tails flicking,
pricked ears, heads jerking,
then off galloping again.

Wind on their backs,
continuously in motion,
in the lighthouse field by the ocean,
all together, almost in formation.
Gypsy training in their breeding;
turning, sinuously weaving,
bold, fast and free,
like white horses on the sea.

Night Owl

Bright moonlight shines,
threading through the pines.
A cold clear night,
an owl in flight.
I stop to look,
ice cracking underfoot.

A scuttering across the way,
a stoop, the prey
between sharp talons;
glimpse of fur, beating wings,
a blur, a piercing cry
and off into the darkening sky.

The Peacock

You preening, prancing fowl,
with your high-pitched miaow.
All show and feathers, fun
to show off to tourists in the sun;
not fit for any other task.

Like an urchin at a masque,
impressive from the front, so refined
but not so dazzling from behind;
your plumage there so foul and fusty,
without its trick of light all brown and dusty.

Considering your dowdy spouse and chick,
could we find anything more comic
than your fan-tailed spread,
your tiny crested head,
and the caterwaul

of your high-pitched mating call?
When your feathers moult
you begin to sulk;
now, with your mincing gait,
fit only for the plate.

Cofion*

'Enter at your own risk',
the notice said,
on the door of this bookshop
by the harbour;
a sea of books piled high,
hiding shelves along the aisles.
Intrigued I entered in,
enquiring after poetry.

'In the literary section,'
I was politely told.
Directed round to where
you could go no further,
where towering, wobbly
book piles met,
I could see that treasures
here were kept.

Rummaging I found, unbound,
a first edition Ezra Pound,
the Ancient Mariner in photostat
and a tattered, battered Rubaiyat;
old memories stacked high.
I could see it was a danger
to browse too deep:
risking ending up beneath a heap.

Poetry can change you, or engulf you.
After recklessly checking
through all the piles across
for a coveted St John of the Cross,

still searching for what I love,
I saw stairs to the floors above
were firmly blocked
by bank on bank of books,

although from outside I had seen
three storeys above, with books
stacked up in all the window nooks.
There must be reasons why
my way was barred;
there would be mysteries beyond my reach.
I could not enter higher,
never to acquire my heart's desire.

*Bookshop beside Tenby Harbour
(Cofion means memories, or souvenirs, in Welsh).

Café Vista

It has to be Café Vista
for the coffee and the vista.
Espresso? Cappuccino?
How can I resist a
latte and a gateau?
Soup or Greek cuisine?
Music evening if you're keen.
Pick up the house guitar
after a few glasses at the bar.
Take a terrace table
if you are able,
or by the window take a pew,
for a sea or harbour view.

Island Foraging

My friend, the herbalist from Myddfai,
spots sorrel, sea spinach,
golden samphire
on the island cliffs.
She loves to forage,
could live in the wild.
Is she descended
from the lady of the lake
and her three physician sons?

When strong winds separate
my Navy friend from Iowa
from her stranded box
of internet-ordered food,
survival trained, she too
looks to forage.
What is it about
these modern women,
still linked to an ancient past?

Echoes

Absorbed in the creative flow,
but unable to let go
of that first memory—
a fragment of time
touched by eternity.
Raw energy flows,
longing for its release
from the tip of the pen;
and the heart still
alive with its radiance.

Lost in the joy
of a fleeting sound,
seeking words to match
the silence that it fills;
far above the normal world,
transported to the harbour
of that other life,
an echo of that other world
awaiting us
the other side of silence.

Pure Music

Rupture in restless time,
beyond the surface of the everyday,
creative flow now constantly unfolding,
beauty giving birth to
subtle music of the mind.
Self-expression breaking forth,
pure music piercing silence,
deeper than awareness.

A rhythm of holy wildness
mirroring that uttered from above,
haunting music of presence
arousing joy, communicating light.
The divine embraced in primal truth,
an icon now in sound,
art linking beauty
from here to heaven above.

Lectio (1)

Looking up from book and pen
to see a little jenny wren;
through the latticed window pane,
the trees all brightly glistening
after summer rain.
Now alert and listening,
to all creation dripping
with the presence
of the living God.
Rapt I sense
the wood alive and singing
of his glory. All in view
reveals that we are nature too.

Lectio (2)

Pink clouds,
the morning sky
still deciding what to do.

Inside, the self falls silent,
as the sound of God's Word
on my tongue is heard.

The ear of my heart awoken,
the eye of my mind is open,
the Word imprints its beauty.

God's Embrace

Finding God without, within,
in self and in the other.
In desire and longing,
responding to the embrace
of God's grace;
love now stirring
deep in the heart.
In the mirror of being
joy awakens;
wonder at God's love
endlessly calling.

Ora et Labora

All is one,
work and prayer,
sea and sky.
At the day's end,
when chant and work
are ended,
the compline bell
rings out across
the silence of the night.
Bright moonlight threads
a beam across the waves;
the spirit alive,
still watching
in the darkened landscape.

'I Thirst'

You thirst, that I
may thirst for you.
Daily you fill
my cup with love,
that I may love
as selflessly as you.
You trod the path
that I must tread,
as faithfully as you.
You seek
to see yourself
at the breaking
of my bread.
You seek my yes
and place a yes
for me to seek,
at depths
beyond all depths.

Prayer of the Heart

By icon and candle,
peace and silence reign;
holy light, flickering
like angels' wings;
the Spirit breathes
the Holy Name;
prayer arises,
fiery tongues
enlighten and inflame;
the soul afire with love
like leaping flames.

Contemplative Prayer

Free fall into naked trust,
deep into the deepest depth;
slipping into the arms
of a God beyond all knowing.
Awareness of his presence
far, far beyond self;
an encounter he decides.

Risking all; nothing withheld
from his transforming love.
Seeking his face,
transformed by grace,
renewed in his embrace;
peaceful my heart,
my joy rimful.

Healing Darkness

Into the shining darkness,
the healing, hidden silence
of the deep heart,
luminous vastness within.

Drawn by love above
to seek within
where God is,
known and unknown.

Delving deep, shedding self
and finding self renewed.
Reaching out,
and ever reaching for

the indivisible kiss,
eternal gift,
where God is
fully known and loved.

Mystical Prayer

Now all time redeemed,
all memories made sense of,
all that was lost and longed for,
all good things as if won back;
both full, and full of longing,
from contact with the world beyond,
pointing to a greater beauty,
where all true hearts
and deepest selves are rooted.
All thoughts exceeded, awakening
the hidden rhythm of the soul.

Frontier of beauty,
between thirst and ecstasy,
where the light of God slips through.
Now loving God with God's love,
seen by God and angels,
divine, invisible embrace;
concealing and revealing mystery,
God's will, his meaning shining through.
Foretaste of heavenly beauty,
restoring goodness, bringing joy.
Like lightning striking to the heart,

the shock of true beauty,
pointing to the naked truth beyond.
Glimpsing the rhythm of the universe,
love, goodness, truth, the One.
Immersed in all creation, filled

by God, restored to wholeness;
transported to love's source,
where music lives, so pure,
so subtle and so fluid;
the still small voice of God's love
singing in the soul.

That Other Life

The world the same now
but different somehow,
catching a new light,
a distant sound that thrills,
attracts me like no other
yet makes me shudder.
He who had always been there
waiting, prompting me to grasp
a new becoming.

Love speaks softly,
asking something new,
now understood as ever there,
preparing for that other life
that waits for me,
as I clearly see
what must be lost,
all like childhood games
that seemed eternal.

On Adoration of the Eucharist
after Watching the Film 'Avatar'

Neural networks
and a tree of souls,
the connectedness
and unity of all life;
how powerful a symbol,
pagan but beautiful,
on Pandora, an alien planet.

How much we take
the Eucharist for granted!
Christ the Son of God,
meaning and unity of all life,
communing with us,
union among us.

God beyond all imagining,
of all possible worlds,
beyond and above all
that can be conceived,
choosing to relate
so intimately to us.

Winter Storm on Priory Beach

Waves climbing the high cliffs;
like a wild child causing mischief,
mocking our sea defences,
throwing rocks and big stones
like confetti on to the jetty;
slicing up concrete,
like a butcher with meat;
cliffs cut like cake,
leaving nothing in its wake.

Venturing out at daybreak
to sand swept from the beach;
in the sea wall there's a breach,
dunes cut as if by a butter knife.
No sign of wildlife;
even gulls wait for the lull
in the storm. Now we've been warned,
on huge respect we all agree
for the awesome power of the sea.

Live Wire

In a dream I woke in sweat from,
my life flashed past;
I was being judged—
the scales weighed down,
my heart against the feather*
(it wasn't going well).
Then I remembered yesterday,
out walking after storms.
I slowed down to notice,
found it strange
to find dead worms
above the sodden path.
Hearing then
a crackling just beneath
where I had all but stepped,
looking up I saw
the wire cut loose,
the fallen tree,
eleven thousand volts
I would have died from.
Stopped dead in my tracks.

*In Egyptian mythology, after death
the heart is weighed in judgement
against a feather.

Kingfisher

Was it our watching,
our waiting,
or the catch and the catcher
that counted?
The mesmerising flash
of green that was seen,
the streak of electric blue,
as the speed of it flew,
swift as a spear,
before the sound hit the ear
of a bird through the water,
less of a bird
than a fisher,
king of this river.

Strangers on the Shore

Among the usual
tidal gathering,
a few curlews,
a lapwing or two,
strangers on the shore
just passing through

on their way elsewhere.
Long-haul travellers
in the risky business
of migration; frequent flyers,
fussy breeders, picky eaters,
wandering the world

or, like the swallow,
in search of endless summer.
Like us they have here
no lasting homeland,
finding only passing joy
instead of what is lasting.

Sunset on the Shore of the Loch

Silence falls.
The sun goes down.
The loch all gold,
all still like glass,
encircled by
the darkening wood.
Tall pines shine bright
like candles
in the setting sun.
My heart is ready,
my soul awake
in the cool silence.
I raise my hands
to sing the evening praise.

The Burning Bush

Enticed, attracted
by a heart poured out;
invited then to enter in
a dialogue of love.
Risk to embrace
love strong as death:
a heart on fire
but not burnt up,
its rapture peace.

God's inner fire,
love's pure light,
transforming hearts.
Take your place,
join in the dance,
delight in truth and light,
in joy be taken up
into love's circle,
hope of eternal beauty.

The Heart Precedes the Mind

When the heart
precedes the mind,
love breeds love
in the hearts
of those who love.

Christ shares our spirit
deep within us,
loves in us
with his love
given to us.

Christ sees himself
in those who gather
what he has sown,
who live with his life
as their own.

Christ is revealed
in what the world conceals.
If we flee from
the odd or underdog,
we flee from God.

We must give our lives
as Christ,
who lives in us, gave his—
gave his earthly life
that we might eternally
share his.

Anger

I killed a man today,
killed him in my heart.
He's dead to my love;
and in the judgement from above
it's for my anger I will fail,
when on the scale
my heart they weigh.

High-Frequency Trading (HFT)*

All the market needs is speed.
Once expert knowledge,
first replaced
by raw young energy,
now by electronic trading,
buying and selling lightning-fast
in microseconds,
between all the stock exchanges
in every time zone of the world.

The algorithm, big data, is king—
robo-traders sifting
through a mass of data,
cashing in each microsecond
on incremental shifts
between the markets.
Are we content to let this process
ratchet up the price of food
when there's enough for everyone?

Create artificial shortages,
so the only way is up?
We used to worry
over crafty rich men
cornering the market
in cocoa beans!
Now we chart the inexorable
ever increasing divide
between the haves and have-nots.

This is the futures market
that adjusts the price of gold
and all our futures, bought and sold;
food prices set to treble in twenty years.
Farmers need insurance, yes,
but let's ban all gambling on food,
stop greedy agribusiness and algorithms
cruelly pushing up the price
of what even the starving eat.

*Computer-generated trading across the
world's stock markets, with the ability
to buy and then sell stocks and shares in
microseconds, using algorithms to make
decisions.

Corpus Christi

'He fed them with
the finest wheat,
with honey from the rock.'

Ps 80:17

Humbled by their hunger,
even then they tested God;
just enough for the day
was what he gave his Chosen,
not enough to store.
Later, the five thousand
ate all they wanted, yet
twelve baskets of scraps remained.
Blessed, broken and shared,
Jesus feeds us with himself,
the living bread, invites us
to become his Body,
to become what we receive,
to offer our poor gift of self
to be transformed, to share.

We who pray for our daily bread
yet store our surplus up,
then question why,
when other people die.
We who have loaves to multiply
create a wilderness for others;
by our greed and exploitation
create an ecological debt
our children and the poor must pay—
the logic of power, not love.

Yet one man who turns to God for answers
can feed a million. If we share,
like 'Mary's Meals' *, as Christ's Body,
we can provide our brother's daily food
and bring about a change of hearts.

Christ is everywhere,
God in bread and touch and word,
a sacrament of this life here,
the mystery that fills,
inviting us to become what we receive,
to realise that all our lives are shared.

* *The Charity that feeds schoolchildren*
a daily meal in poor countries around the world.

Our Fragile Earth

We are born fragile,
uniting to survive,
needing to relate
to create a caring world.
But centuries on we still succeed
in denying, by our greed,
others' basic needs.
All of us are guilty of denying
the rights of the global poor,
even our own children's children,
by our reckless self-indulgence,
by raping the earth's reserves
of non-renewable resources,
ignoring global warming,
still using fossil fuels.

Our fragile earth looks on,
heartbreaking beauty,
provisional mirror of the eternal;
but precarious, in process—
humankind poor guardians of it,
bent on pollution and destruction.
Why can't we see the signs
of our common destiny?
Captured on camera, new life,
seeming flawed and tragic,
is perfect for an instant only.
Here in fragile beauty,
paradise prefigured,
as we wait to be transfigured,
in this path to lasting glory.

Butterfly fluttering
on a fading flower;
above a former war zone,
an eagle soars in might and power.
All in our common home.

Fragile Love

Calming troubled thoughts,
sweet music of whispering leaves;
a leaf boat spins
in the soft wind,
gliding gently downstream.

Spring fragrance,
fragile petals open
to honey bees—
like hearts, created fragile
for intimate encounter.

After spring, so gay and merry,
fragile blossoms fade
on trees of plum and cherry;
fragile hopes begin to ripen
like budding fruit.

Joy, rebirth, time's flow,
the sound of sacred bells;
tear-filled eyes
change to a smile.
Such delicate, fragile love.

Me and My Shadow

As a child at play,
I tried my shadow
to outrun.

Coming to light in prayer,
my shadow self
I tried to overcome.

Dying to self,
in the full brightness of the Son
my shadow and I are one.

A Meeting of Old Friends

Grasping hold of what is past,
looking for clues to what is new,
hoping to start again
where we left off.
There was so much
we shared in common
but now a lifetime intervenes;
so much has happened in between.
Now we have our different stories,
we've lived our different lives.

Now you farm Jacob sheep and llamas:
I'm more into art and drama.
You've given up tennis for the gym:
I've given up the violin.
Yet we try to start again
but stumble on our different memories
of the same events.
It's hard, it hurts
to have old memories proved false.

The Love of a Dying Friend

Your eyes, even now,
speak of happiness to come.
It will break my heart
when in death we part,
but nothing checks, reins in,
the joy of what we have within.

I hold back the tears
to calm your fears,
to let you pass
from love to love.
I know it will never end—
the love of a dying friend.

Love's Remembered Lines

So many years have passed,
I am surprised to see
your face so radiant where
you lie here,
head encased in satin.

I remember
that distant look of joy
and am surprised
to see it now,
although so pale and still.

All the lines now gone,
just as you always lost them
in candlelight, sometimes
in prayer, and when
your gaze was lost in ecstasy.

Laid to rest now,
all that driven life, desire,
loves lost, consumed in fire,
all the heartache, all the pain
of that 'intolerable shirt of flame'.

The Maze*

Those gentle eyes,
soft-bearded mouth defiant,
silent in his iron bed,
staring from a prison blanket.
Front line in the H Block
in the maze of Irish politics.

A hunger striker,
a martyr for the cause
of all of Ireland's troubles,
divisions over flags and creeds,
brother against brother
in the name of unity.

Where is the God
of the Falls Road
these warring tribes invoke?
Where is the God of love and peace?
Still hanging
on the prison wall.

*Prison where Bobby Sands died
(1954-1981)

Faith and Love

If we but believed
what we believe
with joy and holy fire,
that faith and love are one:
drawn near to God
by loving one another,
dying to self
to offer all,
then God would let
himself be found,
in us would let himself
be seen.

Mary

Who else heard the angel
appear or depart
except Mary,
with her listening ear
and ready heart?
Ready to be emptied
for the Word of God,
emptied to be filled
with total love;
formed by God
to give us God
made man,
that man
might be like God.

Everyday Betrayal

Like Judas, He chose us monks
to lead the life in common,
eat at the common table,
share in the common meal,
dip our hands into the Eucharistic dish—
yet we betray Him in our hearts.

Penthos[*]

> *'Joy mingles with sorrow
> like honey in a comb.'*
> St John Climacus

With a heart, broken but open,
that knows God's mercy.
With both heart and will inclined to him,
touched by him who frees us from all sin
that cuts us off from him.

Now serving God with tears,
deep sorrow turning into joy;
joyful sorrow
becoming tears of joy,
joy banishing the sadness.

Holy tears, the gift of tears,
flooding hearts with peace;
tears purifying, marking
the boundary of this present age
with the age to come.

*Compunction

Praxis

He was sent for you and me,
love made visible to set us free.
Christ came from heaven above
to walk the way of truth and love.
He died that we need no longer sin
if we choose to live for him.

On the Cross he took away our sin and shame;
his Spirit fans our love into a flame.
But if you hear his word today,
foot-washing love is not the way
for the lukewarm or the timid,
to walk the way that he did.

The Suffering Servant

Christ's love revealed,
his glory hidden,
overcoming our suffering
in his suffering,
taking all upon himself;
all sin becomes his sin—
being borne by him, forgiven;
all life transformed,
on the cross united with him.

Conformed, becoming one with him,
encountering his hidden presence
in those we meet, the sick,
the stranger, the oppressed.
Confronted by the weakness
of a loving God
who drank that bitter cup,
patiently willing our response,
wanting to raise us up.

At the Foot of the Cross

Filled with sorrow, guilt and shame
to see Christ hanging, racked with pain.
My heart both touched and pierced,
and I now pricked to tears
at what I have chosen to become,
as I look now upon God's Son.
My life held down by sin and self,
the hardened husk of habit.

Because of me he died upon the tree—
all that's beauty crucified for me.
Let my cold heart depart,
I long for heaven above.
Inflamed with love, for love,
the Holy Spirit at the core,
I long to be with Christ once more,
to accept the Word made flesh in me.

Resurrection

Hope not yet abandoned
at the end of night.
Watching and waiting
in the dark-bright-light,
holy fire on the earth's rim.

The sun pours in
over the world's edge.
The gift of joy spills forth,
the eastern sky ablaze
with Easter light.

The Risen Christ

Both desire and gift, his love was;
by his sacrifice, self-emptying love,
he has set eternal life within us.
He is the heartbeat of our lives,
his love is fire alive within us,
living and self-giving,
we in him and he in us,
he the depth that grounds us.

The Risen Christ
unlocks every door
we keep locked;
unlocks them one by one,
as we become
ready to see and touch
what before we would not touch.

Pentecost

The Word on the street
is all about this new life,
where self and sin,
and doubt and fear,
meet up, in prayer,
with holy fire and mighty wind.
A door is opened,
our spirits freed, renewed,
when fear turns into love
and love flows through.

All is shared and held as one;
all united heart and soul,
healing and doing good,
like Jesus, as he said we would.
God's Word changing hearts,
both old and young,
his name in every street,
on every tongue.

The Visitation

In the heat of the struggle
he is there.
He comes to share
our poverty of heart,
to ease our fear and doubt;
teaching us to live
as love poured out,
to share our lives
as he shares ours,
loving each other
in his love,
in love of him.

He lives within us
in our love for one another,
as we reach out to all
who have ever wronged us,
letting go of bitterness,
spreading his mercy
and forgiveness.
As we start to treat
each other as other Christs,
others begin to see
Christ living there within.